work.t

Nathan Ellis

methuen | drama

LONDON · NEW YORK · OXFORD · NEW DELHI · SYDNEY

METHUEN DRAMA
Bloomsbury Publishing Plc
50 Bedford Square, London, WC1B 3DP, UK
1385 Broadway, New York, NY 10018, USA
29 Earlsfort Terrace, Dublin 2, Ireland

BLOOMSBURY, METHUEN DRAMA and the Methuen
Drama logo are trademarks of Bloomsbury Publishing Plc

First published in Great Britain 2022

Cover design: Rebecca Heselton

Cover image © Guy Sanders

A catalogue record for this book is available from the British Library.

Library of Congress Control Number: 2022932017

ISBN: PB: 978-1-3503-3892-0
ePDF: 978-1-3503-3893-7
eBook: 978-1-3503-3894-4

Series: Modern Plays

Typeset by Mark Heslington Ltd, Scarborough, North Yorkshire

To find out more about our authors and books visit
www.bloomsbury.com and sign up for our newsletters.

Nathan Ellis – Writer and Director

Nathan Ellis is a writer for stage and screen. He wrote the text for *No One Is Coming to Save You* (a 'blazing debut', *The Guardian*). In 2020 his play *SUPER HIGH RESOLUTION* was shortlisted for the Verity Bargate Award. He was a member of the Royal Court Invitation Writers' Supergroup 2018–19 led by Alice Birch and Ali McDowall and a member of the BBC Writersroom Drama Room 2021–22. He is represented by Giles Smart at United Agents and is based between London and Berlin.

Emily Davis – Creative Producer

Emily Davis is a producer of theatre and live events. She is Producer at Farnham Maltings and Associate Producer with Poltergeist Theatre. Recent credits include *Ghost Walk* by Poltergeist Theatre (New Diorama Theatre), *work.txt* and *work.txt* online, *i will still be whole (when you rip me in half)* by Ava Wong Davies (The Bunker Theatre) and *Landscape (1989)* by Emergency Chorus (Edinburgh Fringe, National Tour).

Harry Halliday – Technical Production Manager

Harry Halliday is a production manager, sound engineer and Qlab programmer.

Theatre credits include: *work.txt* online (online, with New Diorama Theatre), *work.txt* (VAULT Festival 2020), *X* (Warwick Arts Centre).

Tom Foskett-Barnes – Music and Sound Design

Tom Foskett-Barnes is a composer, sound designer and musical director working across film, theatre and sound art. He scored the Oscar-nominated short documentary *Black Sheep* and Bafta-nominated short *toni_with_an_i*. For stage,

Tom has worked at theatres including the Old Vic, the Arcola, Soho Theatre and The Globe.

In 2016 Tom was Sound and Music Composer in Residence with ROLI as part of the Embedded_Innovate Scheme, and in 2017 Tom was selected as part of the Old Vic 12. Tom's audio documentaries about the UK's queer history, *Living with the Light On* and *Quilts of Love*, were both broadcast by the BBC and produced in collaboration with ICA, the Chisenhale Gallery and NTS.

Tom trained at the Royal College of Music as a Soirée d'Or Scholar, generously supported by a Clifton Parker Award, and was the recipient of a BAFTA UK Scholarship.

Danny Vavrečka – Lighting Designer

Danny trained at the Royal Welsh College of Music & Drama, following a theatre degree at the University of Warwick. Lighting design credits for theatre include: *Jigsaw* (Rose Theatre), *The Moors* (Richard Burton Theatre), *Guys and Dolls* (Warwick Arts Centre Theatre), *X* (Warwick Arts Centre Studio), *Timpson: The Musical* (King's Head Theatre), *Blood Wedding* (Mumford Theatre). Lighting design credits for opera include: *Don Giovanni / Le nozze di Figaro / Il barbiere di Siviglia* (Sherman Theatre).

Ben Kulvichit – Dramaturg

Ben Kulvichit is a performance maker and critical writer. He is co-artistic director of Emergency Chorus. Recent credits include *Mr Jet* (Warwick Arts Centre), *Landscape (1989)* (Edinburgh Fringe, national tour), *work.txt, To Miss the Ending* by idontloveyouanymore (London Film Festival), *Code Silver Code Silver* by YESYESNONO, and *i will still be whole (when you rip me in half)* by Ava Wong Davies (The Bunker Theatre).

Sam Ward – Dramaturg

Sam is a maker, performer and writer. Work includes: *Five Encounters on a Site Called Craigslist* (2017), *insert slogan here* (2018), *the accident did not take place* (2019) and *we were promised honey!* (2022). His work has previously won the Total Theatre Award for Emerging Company and been shortlisted for the Total Theatre Award for Innovation. As a dramaturg/director work includes: *underground* with Babel Theatre (2018), *BINGE* with Mighty Heart (2019) and *work.txt* with Nathan Ellis (2020). His writing is published by Bloomsbury.

Charlotte Fraser – Dramaturg

Charlotte Fraser is an Amsterdam-based director and dramaturg whose work includes *No One is Coming to Save You* (Pleasance, 2018) and *small myth* (VAULT, 2020). Alongside this, she has assisted at The Yard, the Traverse, Theatr Clwyd, Deutsches Theater (Berlin) and on national tours with HighTide, for whom she was resident assistant director 2017–18.

Grace Venning – Dramaturg

Grace is a performance designer based in London and Norfolk. She was a resident design assistant at the National Theatre from 2018 to 2019. In 2019 she was a finalist for the JMK Award with Jocelyn Cox, and for the inaugural Naomi Wilkinson Award for Stage Design with Told by an Idiot. She trained at the Royal Welsh College of Music & Drama.

Antonia Georgieva – Associate Producer

Antonia Georgieva is a creative producer with experience across theatre and media in the UK, the US and Europe. She specializes in subversive new writing and adaptations that challenge the dominant narratives. She is particularly passionate about interdisciplinary performance that engages audiences in novel ways. Recent credits include: *Belvedere* (Old Red Lion), *Echo* (Golden Goose Theatre), *Kitchen* (immersive).

Amy Bethan Evans – Access Consultant

Amy is a London-based playwright and dramaturg originally from Bristol. She was shortlisted for the Kudos Fellowship in 2019 and is under commission at the Royal Court. Her work includes *Libby's Eyes* and *Tinted*.

About Soho Theatre

Soho Theatre is London's most vibrant producer for new theatre, comedy and cabaret. We pursue creative excellence, harnessing an artistic spirit that is based in our new writing roots, the radical ethos of the fringe and the traditions of punk culture and queer performance. We champion voices that challenge from outside of the mainstream, and sometimes from within it too. We value entertainment, accessibility and enjoy a good show. We are a registered charity and social enterprise and our audiences are diverse in age, background and outlook.

We are mission driven and we measure our success in:

- the NEW WORK that we produce, present and facilitate

- the CREATIVE TALENT that we nurture with artists, in our participation work and with our own staff

- the DIVERSE AUDIENCES that we play to and engage

To create theatre we nurture new playwrights, we commission new work and we produce new plays. Writers including debbie tucker green, Chris Chibnall, Theresa Ikoko and Vicky Jones had early work produced at Soho. With comedy and cabaret, we identify, develop and produce exciting new talents and present some of the biggest international stars.

We work beyond Soho taking work to and from the world's major festivals like the Edinburgh Festival Fringe. Our touring work plays across the UK and internationally with strong connections to India, Australia and the US. Our filmed comedy can be downloaded on our digital platform, seen on TV and viewed on international airlines. We're ambitious, entrepreneurial and collaborative and take pride in our strong relationships with commercial partners – but the profits we make go back into supporting our work.

sohotheatre.com | www.sohotheatreondemand.com | @sohotheatre

work.txt

for the workers

The following text is projected, line by line. Anything in italics is not projected.

The stage is set with two microphones on stands and 120 yellow blocks of wood in a pile. There is a printer onstage.

A member of the audience reads the following out
This is a play.
It is performed entirely by us.
Sometimes we will tell the story on our own.
Sometimes we will speak all together.
This is the beginning.

The whole audience
Cool!
This is exciting!
I love it when a performance involves participation
Like in an immersive show
And we're all here

People who work in an office
People who work in an office are here.

People who are self-employed
People who are self-employed are here.

People who feel they are underpaid
People who feel they are underpaid are here.

People who work in the arts
People who work in the arts are here.

People who have nice voices
People with nice voices are here.

Geminis
Geminis are here.

People who are self-starters
People who are self-starters are here.

People who are still working from home all the time
The work-from-homers are here.

Hard workers
The hard workers are here.

People who hate their jobs
People who hate their jobs are here.

People who have been to see the pyramids
People who have been to see the pyramids are here.

People who earn over thirty thousand pounds a year
People who earn over thirty thousand pounds a year are here.

People who earn less than thirty thousand pounds a year
Don't worry!
That's ok!
We aren't bitter.

People who love an experiment with theatrical form
People who love an experiment with theatrical form are here.

People who would rather this were a normal play and are already bored of this and were maybe brought by someone else and are maybe kind of hoping this play will be quite short and were absolutely not informed it was going to be like this
We're here.

A man
Can I ask a question?

The audience
Of course.

A man
What is this all about?
Why are we here?

The geminis (*excitedly*)
That's a great question!

The audience
Well
We are here to tell an important story.
And to have a good time.
To have fun!
To be part of a collective experience.

On today
[INSERT DATE]
At the Soho Theatre
In the room where hit television series *Fleabag* was originally
performed
Which makes it
A cool room[1]

An enthusiastic member of the audience
I hoped it would be like this and that we would be involved
For once!

A pessimist
I'd just like to say
For the record
I'm not having fun yet.

The audience
That's not what we want!
This is supposed to be fun!

The audience
Hm
Hmmmmm
Hmmmmmmmmmmmmmmmmmmmmmmmmmmmmmmmm

The audience
Was that fun?

The pessimist (thoughtfully)
That was very fun.

A woman
I have a question.
Who is in charge?

The audience
I think we are all in charge.

---

[1] Wherever the show happened, there was always a sort of joke about the space and
how cool it was.

The same woman
Someone must be in charge.
There's someone back there pressing the buttons to control
the lights and things.
They must be in charge.

The stage manager
I'm not in charge.

A woman
The ushers, then, I'm very suspicious.

An usher
We don't really even like this kind of thing.
I prefer Netflix.
You could all be watching Netflix now.
Imagine.
It would be lovely if we could just watch Netflix.

The stage manager
I've been making my way through old episodes of *Gilmore
Girls*.
Have you seen it?

People who have watched *Gilmore Girls*
Yes, we've seen it!

The stage manager
I'm on season five.
I like to just have it on in the background.
After I get home.
I'm normally too tired to choose anything I like, so I just put
it on.
I've already seen it but I'm working my way through it
again.
To get to the end again.
And then maybe I'll start it again!
There are so many episodes to get through!

A woman
So, you're not in charge?

The stage manager
No.
In fact, being honest, I'm not even in charge of what I'm saying now.
I haven't even seen *Gilmore Girls*.
It's just what's projected for the stage manager character to say.
I'm not in charge.
I'm just pressing the buttons.

A team-player
Why don't we pretend there is nobody in charge, for now?

The audience
That seems really reasonable.

A self-starter
Is everyone speaking now?
There must be some people who aren't?
Maybe the people who were brought by their friends and don't enjoy experimental theatre?

The people who are not speaking (unspoken)
We're just going to listen.
It's not that we aren't enjoying this.
Or that we're not involved.
Or even that we won't get involved later.
But we're not feeling like being the speakers.
And the rest of you seem to be doing a good job.
Though obviously if you stop, then we'll step in and take over.
Because we're helpful people.

The audience
Great.
That's ok.
If we're in charge, we can do what we like.

A person who feels uncomfortable
So
What happens now?

A member of the audience steps onstage.

They take a block from the pile and place it somewhere else in the space.

A second member of the audience steps onstage, takes a block from the pile and places it somewhere else in the space.

A third.

A fourth.

A fifth.

The entire audience come onstage and place a block of wood somewhere in the space.

They work carefully.

The audience sit back down.

They feel that the thing must be beginning.

Right on cue, there is a beautiful lighting effect.

And music.

The audience admire their work.

A sense of satisfaction.[2]

An audience member with a loud voice
This is the city
A view from above
As if from a high place
A tall structure
A high window of a tall tower
Or a plane coming in to land
It stretches away in front of us
Buildings, roads, tunnels, overpasses, warehouses, stations, skyscrapers.

---

[2] The lighting design does a bit of theatre magic here and turns the blocks, using colour and shadow, into something that really does resemble a city as seen from above.

A map of the city.
On the right is a high tower.
To the left is a train station.
There are cranes everywhere.
This is a setting now.

The audience
As the lights rise,
The city hums with the sound of work.
The city is waking.
Another working day.
Nearly ten million people, all setting about to get
Stuff
Done.

The women
At six fifteen, work is being done, as a million people open
their eyes and immediately reach to check the time on their
phone and see they have an unread message from an
unknown number.

People with long commutes
At six forty, work is being done, and four thousand people realise they missed the point where the sun had risen.

People who don't like Mondays
At seven o'clock, five hundred thousand snooze buttons are hit.

People with children
At seven twenty, work is being done, and one hundred thousand people in one hundred thousand kitchens are letting their coffee go cold as they sweep cereal up from the floor with their bare hands.

People who wear makeup
At seven forty, work is being done, and forty thousand people are disappointed with how their eyes turned out this morning, so are doing them again.

People who drive to work
At five minutes past eight, forty thousand people clench their fists and exhale sharply because of the traffic.

People who forget their password
At eight twenty seven, work is being done, as one million passwords are entered, thirty thousand are incorrect.

People who don't sleep well
At eight forty, work is being done, four million people have found themselves scrolling a website, unsure of how they got there.

The audience
At eight fifty, work is being done
in a tower, somewhere in the city.
As a person arrives at work
this person
on this particular morning
is arriving at their job
back in the office
a space with a hard floor

a high lobby
with a marble floor.
The lobby is busy
a crowd of people arriving at work.

One member of the audience
Then the person in the middle becomes something
different.
They stop
they stand for a moment
and
they lie down
on the hard, marble floor of the lobby.
They lie down
the person, let's give them a name.

A member of the audience picks up the microphone and
says their first name into the microphone.

They spell their first name letter by letter.

They return to their seat with the microphone.

[INSERT NAME] is dressed smartly
they are dressed smartly because it's a [INSERT DAY]
morning and they have to be at their job soon.
They work as a socials and digital communications associate
manager
for a big brand
a brand as big as Coke
as big as McDonald's
something huge.
They work as a socials and digital communications associate
manager for those kinds of brands
and what that means is that they earn more than thirty
thousand pounds a year
to sit in an office and write examples of tweets
or make interesting Instagram content
for a brand as big as Coke
as big as Amazon

as big as Nike.
And then people elsewhere
people who work very part-time
so part-time their jobs are really more a by-the-hour
by-the-task kind of job
[INSERT NAME] tells them what to say, what to tweet
and then they say it.
That is the extent of what [INSERT NAME] does
they come up with things for other people to say about
brands
as big as McDonald's
as big as HSBC
as big as Shell
as big as Apple.
They work hard
they are a hard-worker.

A coffee-drinker
And the story begins when on a [INSERT DAY] morning
this person
a person we're calling [INSERT NAME]
without explanation
lay down on the ground.

A woman
At some point that morning
someone thinks it's strange
let's go to that moment in the story.

Two members of the audience volunteer by raising their
hands.
They wait for two copies of the script to finish printing.
They stand up, walk onto the stage, and take a script each.
They each stand by a microphone stand.
The person in the audience holding the microphone gives
the microphone to the volunteer on the right and they put it
in the microphone stand.
They perform the scene into their microphones.

The audience imagine an office.

an office

The printer prints the scene (the name of the volunteer has been inserted into the scene of the text [INSERT NAME] and is printed, so as to be different every performance):

The scene is projected behind the performers line by line.

A   They were just lying there.

B   Yeah. Just lying in the middle of the lobby?

A   Just lying in the middle of the lobby.

B   What a weird thing to do.

A   That's what everyone was just saying, downstairs.

B   I know, I heard them too.

A   Really weird.

B   Really annoying.

A   [INSERT NAME].

B   [INSERT NAME].

A   Do you think [INSERT NAME] is ill?

B   On strike?

A   Protesting?

B   Fired?

A   Maybe they were just tired, so they lay down?

B   You can't just lie down.

A   Why not?

B   It's a very strange thing to do, don't you think? Do you think?

A   It's a real problem. [INSERT NAME]is the only one with access to the folder.

B   OH! The folder with the files.

A Yes! The folder with all the tweets and the images and everything.

B The most important folder that only [INSERT NAME] has access to.

A That's a real problem.

B A real problem.

A I don't know what we do now?

B Like what work we do?

A Yes. Like how we go on from that problem. Because that's a big problem for me and you because the files are on [INSERT NAME]'s computer, and without them, we can't get anything done.

B The people won't know what to say, if we don't send them the document with the text and the images by five o'clock, then they won't put anything out tomorrow on the social media feeds. All the social media feeds will be blank.

A Does that matter?

B Yes. Definitely.

A Definitely?

B Definitely.

A Oh no!

B I know.

A Oh dear!

B I like what you're wearing.

A Thank you. You look nice too.

B It's nice we get to wear our own clothes to work. That it's informal.

A That is nice. It's nice being back. I was working from home during the pandemic but it's nice to be back I think.

B   You can draft social media posts anywhere. But I think it's nice that we're coming back in. I was sick of being at home. Before I worked here, I was doing the job of the people who maintain the social media feeds.

A   The maintainers?

B   Exactly. I was a maintainer. We didn't get to work remotely. Even during the pandemic. We were in the office. But I was really good at it. so I went up to the manager and I said: I'm really good at this, what will it take to move up to a leadership role. And the manager looked me up and down and they said: That is exactly the kind of entrepreneurial spirit we are looking for.

A   Entrepreneurial is a really difficult word to say, I always think.

B   It is. Entrepreneurial.

A   Entrepreneurialism.

B   Entrepreneurialistic. And the manager moved me to a leadership role the next week. Now I work from home two days a week. And I can take as much holiday as I want. When things are quieter.

A   Normally.

B   Normally. Yes. It's a very fast-paced environment.

A   Not today, though. Not anymore. Not if we can't get those files.

B   Oh, it's a complete and absolute nightmare.

A   So frustrating.

B   That's a nice mug.

A   This mug?

B   Yes.

A   This mug I'm holding in my hand full of coffee? The one with the picture of the pyramids on it?

B   Yes. I really like it.

A   It's not my mug. I just got it out of the cupboard.

B   Have you ever seen the pyramids?

A   No. Have you?

B   Apart from on your mug?

A   Yes, apart from there, have you seen them?

B   I've seen them in pictures. But never in real life. I think it would be cool to see them.

A   I suppose.

B   I think they're really interesting, don't you?

A   I don't know. I haven't thought about it. Why are we talking about pyramids?

B   Well, they're really old, really really old, like, four thousand five hundred years old.

A   That's old.

B   Yeah. And they took ages to build at the time.

A   They would probably take ages to build nowadays too.

B   Exactly. And yet now we just see them as quite strange and really old.

Pause.

A   That isn't that profound a thought.

B   No, but they took so much work, and took so long, so many people –

A   So many slaves.

B   So many slaves, exactly, and I guess I just wonder if at any point while they were building, one of the slaves or one of the architects or anyone, if any of them ever just said: 'what will we do when it's finished?'

A   Don't know.

B   Because now it's been finished for a really really long time, thousands of years, it looks like a lot of work for absolutely no reason.

A   The pyramids are impressive, though.

B   They are. Bet it was satisfying when they got it all done.

A   Yeah. Bet that was a good day.

B   What would you do if you weren't working today?

A   Don't know. You?

B   See all my friends. Read all the news. Listen to every song Celine Dion has ever written. Cook all my meals for the week. Watch the films on the 'One Thousand Films To See Before You Die' book that I have in my house. Go to the gym. That kind of thing.

A   This coffee is nice.

B   It is.

Pause.

A   Ha!

B   What?

A   I've just had a really funny thought.

B   What? Have you?

A   Yes. What do you think would happen if we just lay down. On the ground. Like [INSERT NAME].

B   I don't understand.

A   What do you think would happen?

B   Nothing.

A   We'd hold everything up.

B   Nothing would carry on.

A   We couldn't do it.

B   It'd be stupid.

A   We'd hold everything up.

B   Nothing would carry on.

A   They'd just get someone else in.

B   To do it instead.

A   Besides, it would be boring.

B   If everything was held up no-one would have a nice time.

A   Of course.

B   Of course.

A   I've finished my coffee.

B   I've finished mine too.

A   Shall we sit down?

B   Nice to talk.

A   Nice to meet you.

B   That was fun.

A   Nice to get through it. Hardly made any mistakes!

B   You did great.

The volunteers return to their seats.

The audience
At nine seventeen, work is being done in the lobby, as two security guards bicker about whether this is a matter for the police. It isn't. They call no-one. [INSERT NAME] is still lying there.

People who prefer red wine
At nine thirty, work is being done, and around three hundred thousand people are late, fifty thousand are hungover.

People on social media
At ten fifteen, a thousand printers have inexplicably broken down and forty thousand people are lightheartedly wondering if they would be fired for throwing something hard at a nearby colleague.

Runners
At eleven o'clock, work is being done and people are jogging around parks saying things like 'what a beautiful day'.

Optimists
At eleven minutes past eleven, work is being done, and around a million teas are drunk.

People who share funny things online
Work is being done at eleven thirty, as a very funny person shares a very funny picture of [INSERT NAME] with a very funny caption attached and the picture is shared thousands of times.

Hungry people
At twelve o'clock, work is being done and hungry people are saying things like 'two sugars, please Carol' as they attempt to get through their emails.

People who are paid by the hour
People all over the city are saying things like 'My boss is a dick.'

People who don't like their boss
'My boss is a dick.'

Contemplative people
People are saying things like 'I'm just more productive back in the office.'

A person who recently had Covid
'It feels a bit weird being back with so many people.'

An optimist says
'I'm glad things are back to normal.'

People who get hayfever
At twelve twenty, work is being done, and one thousand doctors simultaneously wish their patients ill but continue to treat them with kindness.

Women
At one o'clock, work is being done, and ten thousand people wearing athleisure are showing each other the picture of [INSERT NAME], still sweaty from their midday barre classes.

People who like art
At twelve fifty, work is being done, in the farthest corner, the farthest building we can see.
An art gallery.
In that art gallery, there is a curator.
Let's go there now.
Two members of the audience volunteer by raising their hands
They wait for two copies of the script to finish printing
They stand up, walk onto the stage, and take a script each
They each stand by a microphone stand
They perform the scene into their microphones

a gallery

The scene is projected behind the performers line by line. The printer prints the scene.

A   I'd like to talk today about truth. About the truth of what life means to me, of what we're doing and why. Of life and death. Of life AND death. And work. Obviously. This is about hard WORK. There has been SO much hard WORK gone into this new. This NEW gallery space, generously funded by Shell, which allows us to explore in dovetail the word of of of express blah the funding the blah blah blah blah.

B   You ok?

A   Sorry, I didn't realise anyone else was here.

B   I was here the whole time.

A   I see that now. Sorry.

B   I stay here the whole time. That's my job. I'm the gallery attendant. What are you doing?

A   I'm rehearsing. I have to do a speech.

B   What for?

A   The room is being renamed.

B   You're the curator?

A   Yes.

B   Congratulations.

A   On what?

B   This room. It's a very nice room. I like the exhibition.

A   Thank you.

B   Workspace. It's an interesting idea.

A   There's a dot.

B   What?

A   Work dot space. There's a dot in the middle. It's . . . The internet. Or something.

B   A lot of people have just been saying 'work space'.

A   Yes, I was told that might happen.

B   I think it's really interesting.

A   That's good. Are you an artist?

B   I studied art but in the script my role is just gallery attendant.

A   It's an important role. Not as important as the curator, obviously, but important!

B   The exhibition makes me think about this thing I saw online, maybe you saw it. It's this person called [INSERT NAME]?

A   No I haven't seen it.

A member of the audience (*shouting out*)   You work here, right? What does this thing here mean? What's it about?

B   Well, everything in this space is about work and space. And this is a piece by an artist from Mexico exploring crafts practices –

A member of the audience (*shouting out*)   So, it's about Mexico?

B   No. It's –

A (*interrupting*)   It's a really interesting piece, actually, exploring the way that work and leisure intersect, the ways beauty and imagination are manipulated –

A member of the audience (*shouting out*)   It looks like blocks of painted wood.

A   It's a lot more than that.

A member of the audience (*shouting out*)   Who are you?

A   I'm the curator. Of the space.

A member of the audience (*reading off the wall, still shouting*) workspace. What's that?

B   Work dot space. There's a dot.

A member of the audience (*shouting out*)   Ok. Where's the best art?

A   Well, it's all world-class, what do you like?

A member of the audience (*shouting out*)   Art. You know, like Art?

A   I'm afraid I don't know what you mean.

A member of the audience (*shouting out*)   Are you patronising me?

A   No.

A member of the audience (*shouting out*)   You are, you're patronising us, you're patronising me and my husband and my family. You think we're too stupid to understand this art and that I want simple art, which isn't true, I just like different things to you, I just use art for different purposes to you. I don't need a gallery to explain what work is because I work already. I don't want to have to work hard in my spare time pretending to like little blocks of wood stacked up on top of each other. I've come a very long way to be here, so that I could look at some really nice art, and feel a bit calmer, and then take a picture to show my elderly relatives when I get home.

A   Well, I think . . .

A member of the audience (*shouting out*)   I'm not finished. I have to be back at work on Monday, real work, not like you do, stood around chatting about thoughts and feelings, about whether work is good or bad or pointless. Of course I hate my job. Everyone does. But you have to work. What else would you do? And the thing is I want to show the people at work that I've been to some proper art on my holiday. Which I think is fine. Isn't it? Isn't that fine? I want to see a Monet.

B There's a Monet on the second floor in the BP Gallery.

A member of the audience (*shouting out*) Thank you.

B I'm sorry about that.

A Don't be. It's fine. They're probably right.

B No.

A They are, they're probably right, the blocks of wood were an error. Whatever. It's not important. I get sent thank-you cards.

B Do you?

A Sometimes. I get sent letters. From people saying how much they like my work.

B That must be nice.

A It is. It makes me think, what I'm doing must be worthwhile.

Pause.

B I don't get sent letters.

A What?

B It was a joke. I'm a gallery attendant, so, obviously I don't get sent letters.

A Of course. A joke. You were talking about [INSERT NAME].

B There are lots of pictures on social media. I'll show you on my phone.

A And then the curator looks at a picture on the attendant's phone of [INSERT NAME] lying down in the lobby.

B   And then the attendant shows the picture of [INSERT NAME] to the curator. The attendant watches the face of the curator, to see if they seem bored or impressed. The attendant talks to the curator about what they think the meaning of the thing might be. They talk about what the significance of [INSERT NAME] is to them, of what that action, which has become a huge sensation on social media, in particular circles, and has strangely taken hold in parts of Asia and South America, might have to say about the world and our place in it. And the curator's face seems to be looking but not really seeing, they aren't speaking, which the attendant thinks must mean they are deeply bored. The important curator isn't engaged. They aren't interested. They can't seem to stop talking. Why did they ever think they should speak to this important person in the first place, when they know they don't like the sound of their voice? When they know that when they get nervous their voice goes all flat and harsh-sounding? The curator must be so bored and angry.

A   The curator is transfixed. They are transfixed by the image of [INSERT NAME]. The image is perfect. A perfect image of flatness, the lack of reality in contemporary life. 'This is perfect.' They hear themself say.

B   What?

A   This is perfect.

B   What is?

A   I love it. We must do it. There's a space here for it. In this gallery. Is it yours?

B   What do you mean?

A   So, you must want this to be a piece in the gallery? It's perfect.

B   This person in the picture isn't me. Their name is [INSERT NAME].

A I've never heard of this artist.

B I think they are just lying down. Apparently. I don't know that much about it.

A I think there's something really interesting in it. I find it very abstract.

B I find it really, really clear.

A Perhaps we could persuade them to move here. We could ask them to move their performance into the gallery, to lie in the gallery.

B I don't think that's the idea –

A Or even better, we could hire actors, to perform the action, to reenact the action.

B Is that –

A No. I've got it. We could request volunteers.

B I –

A We could use this as some sort of engagement project, so that people can engage with the art, requesting people, suggesting to them, that they might engage, by lying down.

B That would be cheaper.

A It would engage people, it would be very engaging. I think you've brought something really interesting. I'm really interested. Would you want to have dinner to talk about it?

B I'm working until the gallery closes.

A What time is that?

B You don't know what time your own gallery closes?

A Of course I do. So, would you like to take the opportunity?

B I'm sorry, I can't.

A I'm offering you a really interesting opportunity.

B   I, I, don't really –

A   I'm offering you satisfaction, an opportunity to be an important artist.

B   I'm –

A   Is it about money? I can offer you money?

B   It's not about the money.

A   What do you want then?

B   I just don't really feel up to it, right now. I don't think I can.

A   You need to make this happen.

B   But.

A   These are unprecedented times. The world is getting going again. We need to make. We need to create. We need to keep moving. We need to pull together, pull your socks up, paint, create, be creative, be productive, make, do, go, build, buy, bring, fetch, carry, work.

B   I'm sorry.

A   [INSERT NAME] will be an important artwork.

The volunteers return to their seats.

A person who is enjoying this
I thought that was really good. Really well-performed.

A man wearing a shirt
I liked the bit where someone interrupted.

A person who hasn't spoken very much yet says this
Can I just say something. I'm still working from home, you know, so I came to this show to try to have fun. To take my mind off things. I love the theatre but this absolutely isn't theatre. Theatre has clever lines and people performing dance routines, and at the very least it has actual actors. Before Christmas I went to see *Mamma Mia the Musical*. Now THAT was proper theatre. They did all sorts of amazing routines and it was funny and you knew the songs, so you could hum along if you wanted. It just made you feel better, whereas this so-called 'play' hardly even has a story.

A person who is finding this play a bit tiresome
In that last scene, I don't understand why the gallery assistant wasn't bothered about money? In real life, that gallery assistant would be really worried about their job. People are really worried about their jobs. I think we should talk about that.

A team-player says this
It said at the beginning that nobody was in charge but all these lines are scripted for us. Even those criticisms were obviously scripted. I'd like someone to say something unscripted now.

The audience feel a deep discomfort.

A few people consider shouting something amusing.

Then, maybe . . .

A young boy dressed as a robot comes onstage and smashes the city to pieces.

A man in the third row could faint.

Everyone in the audience could begin crying simultaneously.

The writer comes onstage and reads out a Guardian article about the four-day working week.

An Alexa sings everyone a song it made up and it's completely amazing.

The audience look under their seats and in an envelope they find their own life-stories, handwritten in a very nice-colour ink.

An actor emerges to do a very beautiful monologue, in a very successful impression of Jeff Bezos.

Everyone gets up and walks out.

Any of those things could happen now.

Or none of those things happen.

The audience could continue to wait.

The audience
I think we should keep going with the story now.

The lights shift and we focus on the city again.

People who don't have kids
At two fifteen, work is being done, a hundred thousand people start flagging and thinking about what they might do with their evenings.

People whose star sign is Pisces[3]
At three o'clock, work is being done, eighteen thousand people blow out the candles on disappointing birthday cakes

People who like swimming
At three twenty, work is being done, someone with a free afternoon is swimming with waterproof headphones in, so that they can listen to a podcast, while they exercise.

---

[3] This star sign was changed to accord with what month the play was being performed, which means if you're really lucky, someone might say this line on their actual birthday.

A woman
At four o'clock, work is being done, and a mother is napping for the first time in four years – she doesn't realise it's been that long but it has.

People who wear glasses
At four-fifty, work is being done and around two hundred thousand people have had their plans fall through.

People who are getting a bit sleepy
At five o'clock, work is being done, as people get up from their office-chairs, stretch their legs, and head home, checking their emails on the way to the lift.

Two volunteers step onstage.

They take the headphones from the usher.

They put the headphones on.

They listen to the instructions.

The volunteers receive instruction.

The audience watch them and wonder what they are being told to do.

The audience give an encouraging thumbs up back to the volunteers.

Everyone feels slightly better.

The audience wonders what secret words are being spoken into the ears of the volunteers.

They wonder if this is going to go wrong.

They think about the mistakes they have noticed so far.

Several members of the audience check the time again in their heads.

Several really need the loo.

Shouldn't have had that beer beforehand.

Too late now.

The volunteers are about to speak.

a cruise ship

The volunteers hear the following through their headphones and repeat it. The scene is projected behind them line by line.

A & B   Hello everyone
The next scene is going to be performed by the two of us.
With these headphones on. The voice in these headphones will tell us what to say.
And then we'll say it. It can be a little difficult when the sentences get longer to keep up with the sense of the sentence because you have to listen and speak at the same time.
Which is.
A skill.

A   I'm ready.

B   I'm ready.

A & B   It is six twenty three pm.
The working day is over.
The world is at leisure.
And we are on a cruise.

A   I think it's going to be a beautiful sunset

B   Where are we going next?

A   Italy's tomorrow.

B   Haven't we had a lovely time?

A   I feel so relaxed. I feel like I could just nod off right here.

B   I had an extremely good bowl of pasta earlier.

A   At the buffet?

B   Yes, at the buffet in the restaurant on the top deck.
It was homemade.
I was thinking I could make homemade pasta my 'thing'.
I could learn to make pasta like that when we're back home and then everyone would be like, '[INSERT NAME]'s dad makes an amazing bowl of homemade pasta.'

A   But you hate to cook.

B   But homemade pasta is impressive.
It's difficult but it's impressive.
If you can do it.
I think it would be nice.
What do you want to do this evening?

A   I don't know.

B   We could do something fun. We could go watch a film in the cinema on deck 16?

A   Go to the theatre in the theatre on deck 10?

B   Absolutely not.
I hate the theatre.

A   A dance class on deck 4?

B   The gym on deck 9?

A   Bowling on deck 20?

B   We could go to karaoke? There's karaoke on deck 2 in the karaoke centre.

A   I'm a bad singer.
You know I don't like singing in front of people.

B   Of course.

A   I've been playing this brilliant game on my phone, while we've been away I got through 15 levels.

B   How many levels are there?

A   Loads.

B   What's the game?

A   It's a game where you just move balls around the screen and pop things. It's brilliant. It's stupid. It's very satisfying.
Our drinks are here.

B   What did you order?

A   A mai-tai.

B   What's that?

A   It's Hawaiian.

B   When were we in Hawaii?

A   Twenty days ago, thereabouts.

B   This is the life, isn't it? I think my favourite so far was Egypt.

A   I don't remember Egypt at all.

B   We've got pictures. I took a nice picture of you with the pyramids. I sent it to [INSERT NAME]. It's nice here.

A   Do you think we're doing well?

B   We're doing really well.
We could have fun?
Make silly noises?

A   What do you mean? How?

B   Bleep bleeeeeep

A   Bleep bleeeeeep

A & B   Bloooopp bloooo000p
bllooooooop blllooooop
blooooopp blooooooop
beeeep beeeep
I am robot
beeeeeep beeeeep

B   There are a lot of people on the deck in front of us. Look at them.

A   Aren't they all dressed so nicely? Everyone has been so nice here.

B   I wonder where they're going?

A   It's almost dinner, probably. Decks 9,10 and 14.

B   I think they like us.
I think we've made a good impression.
We've been really smiley, I think.

A   I'm glad we participated. It's nice to have been part of something. I hope [INSERT NAME] is OK.

B   Shall we call them?

A   Let's call them when we reach land.

B   Italy.

A   I'm going to just try to get to the next level before dinner.

Volunteer B *is instructed to turn away from the microphone and look at the projection behind them, so they are quieter than* **A**.

The sound of the sea begins to rise.

B   Wow! Look at that sunset.
It's beautiful.
So many colours.
Orange

A   Pop

B   Red

A   Pop

B   Green

A   Pop

The sound is now overwhelming their voices.

B   Yellow

A   Pop

B   Ochre

A   Pop

B   Lilac

Volunteer A *is also instructed to turn away from the microphone and look at the projection behind them.*

B   The wind is getting louder

The lines are projected but you cannot hear their voices.

are you cold?

not really

it's peaceful here

I love sunsets on holiday

I don't want to go back

I'm getting hungry

look at the sky

are you still there?

dinner time?

Volunteer B *is instructed to take off their headphones and go and sit back down.*

the sound of the sea at night
the sound wakes me
very late at night
And I can't get back to sleep, so I think I should try to write an email to [INSERT NAME]
But instead I've just been staying up playing this stupid game
I can't seem to get past this one level
And then I go back to sleep and I don't dream about you or me or [INSERT NAME]
I dream about what the next level looks like

Volunteer A *is instructed to take off their headphones and go and sit back down. The projected text continues without them.*

it's a beautiful dream

I'm so happy

it's so nice to be here

what will we do when it's over?

[INSERT NAME]?

everyone has been so nice

dark now

the sea is so quiet

it's so nice to be here

pop

pop

pop

The audience
Every
Night
In
My
Dreams
I
See
You

Karaoke music kicks in and the audience sing 'My Heart Will Go On' together.

The audience
That was fun.
What next?
What happens now?

The end of the working day.

[INSERT NAME] steps onstage

They put on the headphones

[INSERT NAME] receives instruction

A little thumbs up.

They look a little nervous

Of course they do

The audience think about what they have to do after the play

it feels like it's nearly over now

Nearly back to normal

[INSERT NAME] *goes up onstage and is instructed to lie down. They repeat the following. This is projected line by line.*

[INSERT NAME] is still lying on the ground
I've always liked the name [INSERT NAME]
I feel a bit weird that my name has been used so much in the show
In the previous performance the person was called [NAME OF PREVIOUS DAY'S VOLUNTEER].
Wonder what the person will be called tomorrow.
I wonder whether their name will suit them?
I'd like to stop.
I'd like to stop now.
I'd like to stop.
I'd like to stop.
I'd like to stop.
I'd like to stop.
I'd like to stop.
I'd like to stop.
I'd like to stop because I'm tired.
I'd like to stop because I can't think straight.
I'd like to stop because this isn't as entertaining as *Mamma*

Mia the Musical
I'd like to stop because I hate my job.
I'd like to stop because I am having an allergic reaction.
I'd like to stop because I fainted.
I'd like to stop because I want to know where all my money went.
I'd like to stop because I tripped and wanted it to look like I did it on purpose because I was embarrassed.
I'd like to stop because I am angry with my family, with my friends, with my parents for not seeing the signs, for not seeing how unhappy I was.
I'd like to stop because that would be classic me.
I'd like to stop because what will I do when it's finished?
I'd like to stop because I don't eat gluten.
I'd like to stop because I paid for a ticket.
I'd like to stop because this is really hard.
I'd like to stop because I want to dismantle capitalism.
I'd like to stop because I am afraid of bees.
I'd like to stop because I thought we were going to change everything and it's all just the same.
I'd like to stop because sixty giant Jenga blocks cost nineteen ninety nine on Amazon.
I'd like to stop because I am so lonely.
I'd like to stop because I don't like public speaking.
I'd like to stop because I hate people who do hot yoga.
I'd like to stop because I have worked too hard for this.
I'd like to stop because I'm a Sagittarius Gemini Rising.
I'd like to stop because I am going on strike.
I'd like to stop because this career path has disappointed my parents.
I'd like to stop because the war has begun.
I'd like to stop because I feel lost without you.
I'd like to stop because this is stupid.
I'd like to stop because I'm not feeling myself today.
I'd like to stop because it's relatively comfortable on the floor, actually.
I'd like to stop because life is too short.

They stop speaking. The projection continues.

I'd like to stop because I
I'd like to stop because I am
I'd like to stop
I'd like to stop now.

They stay lying on the floor.

The printer will take over the work

The printer begins printing blank sheets until it runs out of paper.

Over the course of the printer's final monologue: a sunset, or perhaps a sunrise.

The printer
The printer's voice is a text-to-voice recording.
The printer will take over from you now [INSERT NAME]
At the end of the working day, everyone else leaves.
[INSERT NAME] is still lying there.
An hour after the end of the working day, several people change their settings to out of office.
Two hours after the end of the working day, the sun has completely set.
Ten hours after the end of the working day, a car alarm goes off outside.
Thirteen hours after the end of the working day, work begins again.
Three days after the end of the working day, a very good post on Twitter is cause for celebration.
Four months after the end of the working day, they make everyone change their passwords.
A year after the end of the working day, [INSERT NAME]: the play opens on Broadway with James Corden playing every part.
Two years after the end of the working day, the one hundredth Covid variant is discovered in Lincolnshire and a rainbow-coloured post-box is installed as a tribute.
Three years after the end of the working day, the two office workers die while learning to paraglide.
Five years after the end of the working day, someone says it is all back to normal now and someone else says yes.
Nine years after the end of the working day, the curator has a breakdown and becomes a carpenter.
Twelve years after the end of the working day, Keira Knightley plays Karl Marx in a five-film adaptation of *Das Kapital*.

Fifteen years after the end of the working day, we work very hard and global temperatures have risen by two degrees above pre-industrial levels so we have a party.

Forty years after the end of the working day, McDonald's changes its name to the archy archy gold gold.

Fifty years after the end of the working day, and the final ancient tree in the Amazon is cut down.

Eighty years after the end of the working day, the humans relocate underground due to the extreme surface heat.

Two hundred years after the end of the working day, and Jeff Bezos dies on Mars.

Five hundred years after the end of the working day, and all the humans are dead. Work doesn't notice and keeps on keepin on.

One thousand years after the end of the working day, aliens land on earth to take a picture with the pyramids, even though they aren't that impressed by them up close.

Four thousand years after the end of the working day, nature stays late at the office again.

One hundred thousand years after the end of the working day, the magnetic poles go freelance.

Two hundred thousand years after the end of the working day, sound gets put on a zero-hours contract.

One million years after the end of the working day, God tries lateral thinking.

Fifty million years after the end of the working day, evolution leans in.

One hundred million years after the end of the working day, light impresses the MD.

Five hundred million years after the end of the working day, language feels like a winner.

A billion years after the end of the working day, colour smashes the interview.

Three billion years after the end of the working day, gravity does a Myers-Briggs test.

Five billion years after the end of the working day, space dresses for the job it wants.

Ten billion years after the end of the working day, the

universe makes partner.
One hundred billion years after the end of the working day,
time defects to the competition.

Applause.

Acknowledgements

There are so many people to thank for having made the play possible:

My amazing family and my brilliant friends.

My wonderful and kind agent Giles Smart, Dom O'Hanlon and the team at Methuen. SheShePop, the company whose show *Oratorio* inspired so much of the form of the play. The lovely Antonia Georgieva, Danny Vavrečka, Charlotte Fraser, and Grace Venning. The team at The Yard, Gill Greer, Lakesha Arie-Angelo and everyone at the Soho, Meg Hird, Eleanor Turney, Guy Sanders, Eve Allin, Sam Osborne, Sir Ian McKellen, Matt Maltby, Nick Oliver, Andy McNamee, Emma Baggott, Tim Crouch, and, as always, David Byrne at NDT.

The dramaturgs Sam Ward and Ben Kulvichit, whose extraordinary brains were there right at the very start when I was stressing over which giant jenga blocks to buy.

Tom Foskett-Barnes for lending his considerable talents to the project. He's the best around – even if he is appalling company.

Harry Halliday, who agreed to work on a very technically complex play with a man who was trying to make it work using powerpoint. He was endlessly patient as he fixed problems I had caused and found honest-to-god miraculous things to do with a QLab file. I am so grateful he has not yet got sick of me or my rewrites.

Producer Emily Davis – I actually don't know if it's possible to express how much she's given to the play, but 'producer' only covers a tiny fraction of it. Her creativity and kindness are imbued in every beat of *work.txt*, and the play is deeply indebted to her. Emily's boundless enthusiasm and love of theatre made working on it – even when struck down by a nearly two-year Covid hiatus – a complete pleasure for me. I am fortunate to count her as a collaborator and a friend.

Finally, at the risk of sounding a bit of a knob, I want to thank the audiences who performed and continue to perform the play. *work.txt* asks a lot of the people who choose to come see it, and I think that in watching the show as an outsider to the audience, I get to see people at their best: getting involved, being brave, trying to make the thing work, so everyone can enjoy it. I dedicate this play to them.

Printed in the USA
CPSIA information can be obtained
at www.ICGtesting.com
LVHW020748181024
794056LV00008B/937